Kim

Nature's Footprints

IN THE AFRICAN
GRASSLANDS

By Q. L. Pearce and W. J. Pearce

Illustrated by Delana Bettoli

Silver Press

ACKNOWLEDGMENT

*Special thanks to Tony Valenzulla, Curator of
Mammals at the Los Angeles Zoo, for his assistance.*

*For my sister-in-law
Grace
—D.B.*

10 9 8 7 6 5 4 3 2 1

Library of Congress Cataloging-in-Publication Data

Pearce, Q. L. (Querida Lee) Nature's footprints in the African grasslands / text by Q. L. Pearce and W. J. Pearce ; pictures by Delana Bettoli. p.   cm. Summary: The reader is invited to follow animal tracks and observe how grasslands animals of the Serengeti protect, feed, and care for their young. 1. Grassland fauna—Africa—Juvenile literature.   [1. Grassland animals—Africa.   2. Parental behavior in animals.   3. Animals—Infancy.   4. Animals—Habits and behavior.]   I. Pearce, W. J.   II. Bettoli, Delana, ill.   III. Title.
QL336.P43   1990
599.09678'27—dc20
89-39510
CIP
AC
ISBN 0-671-68831-6   ISBN 0-671-68827-8 (lib. bdg.)

A Note to Parents

NATURE'S FOOTPRINTS is a read-aloud picture book series that introduces children to a wide variety of animals in a unique, interactive way.

Ten animals are presented in pairs, along with a sample of each animal's footprints. In the scene that follows, the animals can be found by tracking the paths of their footprints, thereby building your child's observational skill in a lively, fun format.

Detailed illustrations and text provide more information about the animals. Encourage your child to point out details about the animals and their environment.

Accompanying the NATURE'S FOOTPRINTS series is the NATURE'S FOOTPRINTS FIELD GUIDE—a handy, colorful reference guide that teaches children even more about the animals in this series.

THE ELEPHANT

The elephant and her calf live in a group called a herd.

The mother protects her baby.

She chases away other animals that might hurt her young one

THE LION

A baby lion is called a cub.

The lioness hides her cubs safely in the grass.

She feeds them milk many times each day.

Baby elephants are the world's biggest babies.

Follow nature's footprints.

They will lead you to the biggest baby elephant.

A family of lions is called a pride.

Follow nature's footprints.

They will lead you to the leader of the pride.

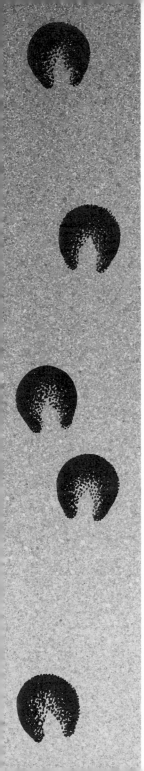

THE ZEBRA

A mother zebra is called a mare.

A baby zebra is called a foal.

The mare feeds milk to her foal until it can eat grass.

THE GIRAFFE

The giraffe is the world's tallest animal.

The mother shows her baby how to reach for leaves to eat.

She shows her baby how to stoop for water to drink.

The father zebra, or stallion, guards the family.
Follow nature's footprints.
They will lead you to the brave stallion.

The giraffe calls softly to her baby, *"Mooooo!"*
Follow nature's footprints.
They will lead you to the hidden giraffe.

THE BABOON

A young baby baboon clings to its mother's belly.

An older baby rides on its mother's back.

At night, they all sleep safely in the treetops.

THE OSTRICH

The father ostrich digs a nest in the sand.

The mother ostrich lays her eggs in the nest.

Both parents take turns sitting on the eggs to keep them warm.

Baboons travel in groups called troops.

Follow nature's footprints.

They will lead you to the mother with the youngest baby

Ostriches find food for their newborn chicks.

Follow nature's footprints.

They will lead you to the busy ostrich.

THE CHEETAH

The mother cheetah feeds milk to her newborn cubs.

When the cubs are old enough, they eat meat.

Cubs hide while their mother hunts for food.

THE ANTELOPE

Antelope mothers usually have one baby at a time.

In a large herd, there may be many babies.

Each mother knows her baby by its scent.

When cheetah cubs are old enough, they learn to hunt.
Follow nature's footprints.
They will lead you to the hunting cub.

An antelope baby can run and leap soon after it is born.
Follow nature's footprints.
They will lead you to the jumping antelope.

THE JACKAL

Baby jackals are called pups.

They are born in a cozy burrow.

Both father and mother jackal care for the pups.

THE LEOPARD

A mother leopard may have two or three cubs.

She cares for them during the day and hunts at night.

The cubs hide until they are old enough to hunt, too.

Jackals hunt in a group called a pack.
Follow nature's footprints.
They will lead you to the fastest jackal.

Young leopards learn to climb trees.

Follow nature's footprints.

They will lead you to the fearless leopard cub.